Hieroglyphs

The Writing of Ancient Egypt

Norma Jean Katan

with
Barbara Mintz

Published for the Trustees of
the British Museum
by British Museum Publications

Published by British Museum Publications Limited
46 Bloomsbury Street, London WC1B 3QQ

British Library Cataloguing in Publication Data
Katan, Norma Jean
Hieroglyphs.—Rev. ed.
1. Egyptian language—Writing, Hieroglyphic
I. Title II. Katan, Norma Jean. Hieroglyphs, the writings
of ancient Egypt III. British Museum. *Trustees*
493'.1   PJ1097

ISBN 0-7141-8060-2

Front cover   Detail from a list of Kings' names carved in hieroglyphs. Found in the temple of Ramesses II at Abydos.

Designed by Grahame Dudley

Typeset in Linotype Palatino by Peter MacDonald

Printed in Great Britain at The Bath Press, Avon

CONTENTS

Introduction

Hieroglyphs are the signs or letters used in ancient Egyptian writing. There are over seven hundred of these signs, and each one is a picture of something familiar to the ancient Egyptians – such as an old man leaning on a stick, a cow suckling her calf, a clump of papyrus, or

1. Personal possessions were often inscribed with the donor's name. This wooden cosmetic container for eye make-up belonged to the Overseer of Works and Scribe Ahmose. 18th Dynasty, reign of Hatshepsut to Tuthmosis III, about 1500-1450 BC.

a boat. Hieroglyphs were carved and painted on the walls of tombs, temples and pyramids, as well as on statues. They were even used on everyday things and personal possessions (1).

The ancient Egyptians called their writing 'words of the gods', because they believed that Thoth, the god of learning, had invented writing. The word 'hieroglyph' was first used to name these signs after 300 BC, when the Greeks in Egypt saw them carved on the temple walls. In Greek *hiero* means 'holy' and *glyph* means 'carving'. After the Greeks, under the command of Alexander the Great, took control of Egypt in 332 BC, Greek became the official language of Egypt, spoken by the Greeks themselves and used for official documents. But the ancient Egyptian language continued to be spoken and its scripts written by the Egyptians for at least another seven hundred years. Only then was the knowledge of how to read hieroglyphs lost.

For the next fourteen hundred years hieroglyphic writing remained a mystery that no-one could solve, though many people tried. The key was finally discovered in 1799 at a place known as Rosetta. Some soldiers of Napoleon's army, while working on the construction of a fort, found a slab of stone quite unlike anything else they had seen in Egypt (2). It was about four feet high and was covered with what seemed to be three completely different kinds of writing. One of the texts was written in Egyptian hieroglyphs. Scholars soon found that the second of the three texts was written in demotic, an extremely cursive script that developed around 700 BC from hieratic; the latter is itself a cursive version of hieroglyphic writing. Although the Egyptian scripts could not be read, the third inscription was in Greek and could therefore be translated. Scholars soon realised that all the texts said the same thing, so they had finally found a way to decipher Egyptian hieroglyphs.

The man who eventually solved the mystery was a young Frenchman named Jean François Champollion. He had always been fascinated by languages. When he was only eleven he was shown some hieroglyphs and told that no-one in the world could read them. He im-

6

mediately made up his mind that he would be the one to decipher them. He studied the Rosetta Stone for twenty years and learned eleven languages, including Greek and Hebrew.

2. The Rosetta Stone with the same text in three scripts: hieroglyphs, demotic and Greek, dated 27 March 196 BC. The text is a decree passed by an assembly of priests conferring honours on King Ptolemy V. Basalt.

In the Egyptian hieroglyphic text certain signs were enclosed in ovals, called cartouches, like this:

Scholars had suspected that these cartouches contained the names of the rulers, and that the oval ring around them was to show that they were especially important. It was known that the name of Ptolemy appeared frequently in the Greek text, so it seemed possible that the signs enclosed within the oval rings in the Egyptian text might stand for the same ruler (3). The question was settled in 1822, when Champollion was made aware of a cartouche on an obelisk which was thought to contain the name of Cleopatra. Until this time many scholars had believed that each sign represented a picture. Champollion recognised that some signs in the two cartouches were the same, and he finally connected each of the signs with a sound instead of a picture. By comparing the signs he was able to confirm that the cartouches did contain the names of Ptolemy and Cleopatra. This was the breakthrough needed to begin the scientific decipherment of hieroglyphs.

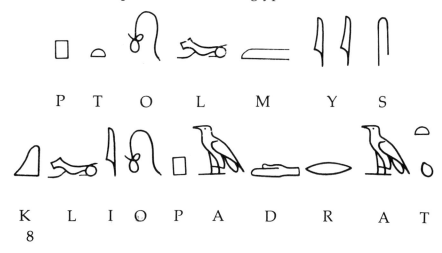

3. *Detail of lines 3-8 of the hieroglyphic section of the Rosetta Stone, showing the name of Ptolemy written in a cartouche.*

Hieroglyphs and magic

Hieroglyphs meant more to the ancient Egyptians than simply a method of writing. They also had another purpose – a magical one. They were not just used to spell out words, but could represent the actual object itself. In some tombs hieroglyphs that represented evil animals were drawn without legs or heads, or chopped in half, or even nailed down so that the 'animals' could not eat the food that was left in the tomb for the dead person to eat in the next life (4). The hieroglyph of a snake was sometimes left whole, though, because it would not be interested in eating human food.

9

4. *Inscriptions inside the schist sarcophagus of Princess Ankhnesneferibre, showing the snake determinative (see p. 9) of the evil serpent Apep pinned down by knives (centre left). From Thebes; 26th Dynasty, about 525 BC.*

5. *Erased cartouches and figure of Queen Hatshepsut running before the god Amen-Re in his form of fertility god. Painted sandstone. In the temple of Amen-Re at Karnak; 18th Dynasty, about 1503-1482 BC.*

Words were so powerful to ancient Egyptians that they were sometimes used as a way of making a person disappear. When Queen Hatshepsut died in 1470 BC, her stepson, Tuthmosis III, who had always hated her because she prevented him from ruling as Pharaoh, took revenge on her by chiselling her name off all her temples. To him, and to everyone else, Queen Hatshepsut completely disappeared from history when her name and pictures were scratched out everywhere (5). It was as if she had never existed. The name of Tutankhamun,

6. *Detail of the inscription of the granite base of one of the lions from Gebel Barkal, showing how the cartouches containing the names of King Tutankhamun have been obliterated. 18th Dynasty, reign of Amenophis III, about 1380 BC.*

too, was often obliterated by later kings (6), because he was connected with the religious heresy begun by King Akhenaten, who tried to establish a form of the sun-god as supreme god in opposition to the empire-god Amun.

11

Another example of the power of hieroglyphs is demonstrated in a relief (7) from a doorway showing an *ankh* sign, the sign of life, held up to the nose of King Psammetichus III. Ancient Egyptians believed that the nose was the 'seat of life'. To destroy an enemy forever was a simple matter – it could be done by smashing the nose of a statue or on any other representation of the person. To hold the *ankh* sign to King Psammetichus' nose magically guaranteed his eternal life.

7. Scene on a door-jamb showing an ankh *sign held to the nose of King Psammetichus* III *by the god Amen-Re. Sandstone. From the temple of Osiris at Karnak; 26th Dynasty, 526-525* BC.

The Egyptians believed in a life after death, which they hoped would be like their life on earth, only better. Early in his or her lifetime every Egyptian who was able planned and built a tomb with the help of an architect, masons and artisans. It was furnished with everything the person would need for a comfortable afterlife – food, furniture (8), clothing, jewellery and games. It was thought that the activities enjoyed or carried out

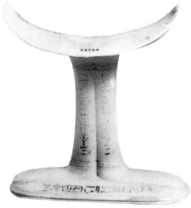

8. An alabaster headrest inscribed for its owner, the high official Meryrehashtef. From his tomb at Sedment; 6th Dynasty, about 2200 BC.

9. Miniature bronze yoke and bags for carrying grain, named for their owner Hekareshu. From Abydos; 18th Dynasty, about 1400 BC.

during the dead person's lifetime would continue in the afterlife: everyday objects, or models of them (9), were provided for this purpose. Agricultural work would still be required, but this duty could be avoided by placing in the tomb a *shabti* (10), a model figure who would magically substitute for the dead person.

10. *A painted limestone* shabti *carrying broad and narrow-bladed hoes and seed-bags for use in the afterlife. The text names the owner as a Musician-priestess of Amen-Re at Thebes, but her name has been obliterated. 18th Dynasty, about 1400 BC.*

11. Copy of a wall-painting showing the nobleman Nakht hunting birds and spearing fish in the marshes. Painted plaster. Tomb no. 52 at Thebes; 18th Dynasty, about 1420 BC.

It was also hoped that other, more pleasurable, activities would continue. The wall-painting in 11 shows Nakht, a scribe of the granaries during the 18th Dynasty. Nakht had this scene painted showing himself hunting birds and spearing fish to make sure that the pleasure of this sport would magically continue for him in the next life. His name was written in hieroglyphs on the painting like this:

Like all Egyptians Nakht believed that if his name was written down, both he and his name would continue after his death.

15

Often the objects included in the tombs were represented in paintings (see the sandals painted in the inside of the coffin of Gua, 17) or listed in hieroglyphic texts. This acted as an extra security measure in case the tomb was robbed of its contents – the mere depiction of an object was thought to guarantee that it would be provided magically in the afterlife. Hieroglyphs therefore had a special force in that not only was the object listed in a magic text but the sign for the object's name was often actually a picture of it.

All tombs also contained slabs of stone, called stelae, on which words of magic power were carved or written. Stelae were placed either against walls or built into them. They came in various shapes and sizes, and were

12. Limestone stela of the sculptor Userwer, depicted with his wife, parents and sons and daughters, who are presenting offerings to him. 12th Dynasty, about 1900 BC.

used for a variety of purposes. Funerary stelae vary greatly, but they always showed either the dead person receiving offerings or an offering formula. Since the ancient Egyptians believed that they needed food for

13. *Painted limestone stela of the priest Ity, dated to the fourteenth year of King Sesostris I. Ity is shown sitting with his wife before an offering table while a son offers birds. Below, the deceased is shown again with two daughters. 12th Dynasty, about 1957 BC.*

their afterlife, they made a written contract during their lifetime with priests and relations, who agreed to bring the food to the tomb after the person had died and place it on an offering table. Many funerary stelae show the family of the dead person making offerings to the deceased (12,13).

Rahotep was a high official during the 4th Dynasty, around 2550 BC. On his stela (14), facing Rahotep, is an offering list which names the things he needed for his afterlife. The pictures of food in the offering list were not just pictures: they were signs that could magically become real food in the next life if, by chance, real food were not left on the offering table. The name and profession of the dead person were always given in the offering list, along with a picture of the person.

14. *Limestone stela of the King's Son and high official Rahotep, who is shown seated before an offering table and list of offerings. From Meidum; 4th Dynasty, about 2550 BC.*

15. *Top of a limestone stela showing the High Priest of Ptah Pasher-Ptah kneeling before an offering table, behind which stand Osiris and other deities. From Saqqara; Ptolemaic Period, reign of Queen Cleopatra VII, about 41 BC.*

Below is another offering list from the 5th Dynasty, two hundred years later than Rahotep's. The offering list consists for each element of two signs: the first one is a number, the second is the offering.

 is the hieroglyph for 1,000. After the 5th Dynasty it became a standard formula:

19

1,000 loaves of bread

 1,000 jugs of beer

 1,000 cattle

 1,000 geese

1,000 alabaster jars

 1,000 pieces of cloth

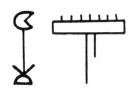 all things

 good

[and]

 pure

Another type of stela is called a false-door stela, because the lower part is shaped like a doorway (16). It was set into a wall within the tomb so that the spirit of a dead person could return from the afterlife through the 'door' and find the food that his or her relatives or the priests had left. The dead person's spirit could then return through the 'door' to the other world.

Some of the texts in Egyptian tombs were prayers and hymns to the gods which were spoken or chanted at funerals to help the dead person on his or her journey

16. Detail of a painted false-door stela in limestone of the Royal official Kaihap; his wife, children, other high officials and offering-bearers are also depicted. From Saqqara; 5th Dynasty, about 2350 BC.

through the underworld on the way to heaven. The earliest of these texts that we have are prayers for rulers of the Old Kingdom, called *Pyramid Texts*, because they were written on the walls of burial chambers in pyramids. The *Pyramid Texts* assured any ruler who used them of a safe place in the afterworld. With the help of these writings he or she would be able to defeat all monsters and demons that occur on the journey to heaven.

Another version of these spells was used during the Middle Kingdom. Because they were written on the inside of wooden coffins and on coffin lids, these inscriptions are called *Coffin Texts* (17). The *Pyramid Texts*

17. Coffin texts painted inside the wood inner coffin of the Physician Gua. Beneath the row of large hieroglyphs are depicted granaries and the deceased's sandals. From El-Bersha; 11th Dynasty, about 2050 BC.

could only be used by kings and queens, but the *Coffin Texts* could be used by noblemen and other important people. They gave protection against hunger, thirst and the dangers of the underworld. They also gave the dead person the power to change into whatever form he or she wanted to take in the next life and guaranteed that the life would be a happy one.

In the New Kingdom there was a third version of these magical texts, which was for sale only to well-to-do Egyptians, as it was expensive. It is believed that priests sold them at temples. We call them *Books of the Dead*, though they are not really books. They are a collection of religious sayings and magical texts, some of which were read and chanted during funerals. These prayers and spells were written on papyrus or leather which was placed in the tomb, sometimes put into a wooden box decorated with a statuette of the god Ptah-Sokaris-Osiris or laid within the coffin with the mummy. Their purpose was to guarantee a safer passage through the underworld and a happy afterlife for the dead person.

There are nearly two hundred 'chapters' (or sections) of the *Book of the Dead*, but as far as we know, no existing papyrus contains all the chapters. Each person chose those chapters that he or she particularly wanted or could afford to have copied. Members of royal families, priests or scribes sometimes bought expensive copies and had them illustrated by well-known artists. Other copies were prepared with blank spaces left, so that the name of the person who bought one could be added later. During the New Kingdom texts from the *Book of the Dead* were also painted on the walls of the tombs of noblemen. Sometimes four bricks inscribed with short texts from the *Book of the Dead* were placed in niches in the four walls of the tomb chamber, to prevent the dead person's enemies from attacking the body. These enemies could come from the north, south, east or west, and so four bricks were needed to keep them away.

24

The craft of the scribe

The people who knew how to read and write hiero-glyphs were called scribes. Since few Egyptians knew how to read and write, those who did were highly re-spected. It was the greatest ambition of many parents to have their children educated to become scribes. We know that some girls were taught to read and write; certainly princesses were. Indeed, writing equipment belonging to two of King Akhenaten's daughters has been found. It is unlikely, however, that girls from less important families were taught.

As a rule, boys in ancient Egypt entered the same profession as their fathers; a baker's son became a baker and a sandalmaker's son became a sandalmaker. Only by learning how to read and write hieroglyphs could a boy break from the family tradition, and by becoming a scribe he was able to enter the higher ranks of society.

The schooling of a scribe began at an early age and was completed at sixteen. To become a scribe meant ten to twelve years of hard training. The first step for some was to enter a special school at a royal palace. There the boy was taught with the children of the royal family. Children from noble but not necessarily rich families were sent to schools attached to temples, where they were taught by priests. Children from poor families, if they were talented, were instructed by the village scribe, who usually taught his own children and those of his relatives.

Scribes' school was a long and difficult course of study. At first the young apprentice had to memorise the most commonly used hieroglyphic signs, of which there were several hundred. He would practise writing with a brush on pieces of pottery or limestone, called ostraka (18), and wooden boards covered with a white coating called gesso, a mixture of plaster and glue. When a student became more skilled at writing hieroglyphs he was allowed to use papyrus, which is a paper-like material made from the pith inside the stem of the papyrus plant. Beginners could not use papyrus because it was too expensive.

18. Painted ostrakon in limestone used by a scribe to practise the hieroglyphs of a lion's head and ducklings. 20th Dynasty, about 1150 BC.

19. Wood writing palettes; scribal palette of King Amosis I, still with its brushes; painter's palette with depressions for many different coloured cakes of paint belonging to the Chief Royal Steward Meryre. 18th Dynasty, between about 1550 and 1450 BC.

The scribe's writing tools (19) consisted of a palette that held two cakes of ink, one red and one black; a pot of water to moisten the ink; brushes of various sizes; and a brush holder. The scribe made his brushes by cutting lengths of rushes and sucking one end to make it soft. These tools were light and easy to carry (20).

The young scribe learned to write not only hieroglyphs, but also hieratic, which was the form of cursive writing. In hieratic script (21) the forms of the hieroglyphic signs were simplified and many were joined as in our handwriting. Hieratic differs from hieroglyphs in the same way that our handwriting differs from printed letters. Hieratic was used mainly for everyday business matters.

20. Detail from the limestone stela of the Royal Libationer Iry, showing scribal equipment carried over the shoulder of the Scribe Kanefer. Notice the detailed hieroglyph depicting scribal equipment (below the elbow of the large figure). From Giza; 5th Dynasty, about 2400 BC.

21. Sheet of the Great Harris Papyrus containing King Ramesses III's concluding prayer to Amun: a superb example of scribal hieratic of the Ramesside Period, 20th Dynasty, reign of Ramesses IV, about 1166 BC.

22. Sculptor's trial piece showing an exercise for carving the hieroglyph t. Limestone. From Abydos; 19th Dynasty, about 1300-1250 BC.

By copying and recopying many different types of letters and texts the young scribe became educated in literature, religion, mathematics and medicine. Scribe school was not easy, as we learn from a text on a papyrus: 'Spend no day in idleness or thou wilt be beaten'. However, it must have seemed worth the effort. In another papyrus, a father tells a son how much better it is to be a scribe than anything else:

It is greater than any other profession. There is nothing like it on earth.

I have seen a coppersmith at work at his furnace. His fingers were like the claws of the crocodile and he stank more than a fish.

The jeweller . . . when he has completed the inlay work of amulets, his strength vanishes and he is tired out.

The barber shaves until the end of the evening. But he must be up early . . . He takes himself from street to street to seek someone to shave. He wears out his arms to fill his belly.

The potter is covered with dirt. His clothes . . . stiff with mud, his headdress . . . of rags.

I shall describe to you the bricklayer. His kidneys hurt him.

The weaver inside the weaving house is . . . wretched . . . He cannot breathe the air. If he wastes a single day without weaving he is beaten with fifty whip lashes . . . He has to give food to the doorkeeper to allow him to come to the daylight.

The arrow maker is completely wretched.

The furnace maker, his fingers are burnt . . . his eyes are inflamed because of the heaviness of the smoke.

The washerman launders at the riverbank near the crocodiles.

After all this, the father tells the son: 'See, I have placed you on the path of God.'

After a boy's education as a scribe had been completed, he could become an accountant, a doctor, a priest, a granary foreman, a cattle foreman, a foreman of weavers, a foreman of craftsmen, a foreman of sculptors, or a private secretary to the king or a nobleman. A quotation from the Papyrus Anastasi 4 (BM 10249) shows the important and privileged position scribes held in Egypt: ' . . . the scribe directs every work in the land . . . for him there are no taxes . . . he payeth tribute in writing'.

23. Quartzite statue of the Chamberlain of the Divine Adoratrice Pes-shu-per, depicted as a scribe with papyrus unrolled on his lap and scribal equipment over his shoulder. 25th Dynasty, about 700 BC.

30

Reading the hieroglyphs

Hieroglyphs show pictures of animals, human beings or objects that were familiar to most people in ancient Egypt (24). In the very beginning, around five thousand years ago when hieroglyphs first appeared, these pic-

24. *Limestone relief with the hieroglyph of a quail chick representing the sound* w *or* u. *New Kingdom, about 1500-1100* BC.

tures represented just what they showed. A picture of a mat was meant to be read 'a mat'.

25. *Limestone relief with the hieroglyph of an owl representing the sound* m. *New Kingdom, about 1500-1100* BC.

At about the same time, in 3100 BC, when King Narmer became the first king of Upper and Lower Egypt, some of these pictures or signs came to stand for the sound that the original Egyptian word began with, and these became the twenty-four alphabetic hieroglyphs. The sign for 'mat' now stood for the sound p, because that is what the Egyptian word for mat began with. For instance, the hieroglyph which shows an owl (25) stands for the letter 'm', with which the Egyptian word for owl began, and it sounds like our m as in 'mother'. Below are the twenty-four alphabetic hieroglyphs; beside each is the name of what it represents and the sound for which it stands. All of them are consonants, as the Egyptians did not write vowels. In order to write them in English they must be expressed in our letters. We call this transliteration. The first few signs of the alphabetic hieroglyphs can be transliterated as vowels, since they are really weak consonants, or 'semi-vowels'. The English 'y', for example, can be a vowel as in 'baby' as well as a consonant as in 'yes'.

a vulture

A as in 'ah'–
To transliterate this, we use the phonetic symbol 3 representing a glottal stop and pronounced as in 'bottle' when spoken by a Cockney.

a flowering reed

I as in 'sit'

two flowering reeds

has two sounds: Y as in 'baby'; Y as in 'yes'

an arm and
a hand

A as in 'bark'
(There is no real equivalent to this sound in English. Phonetically it is written ʿ; the closest sound is the *ayin* of semitic languages.)

a quail chick

has two sounds: W as in 'won', OO as in 'move'

a foot

B as in 'bat'

a mat

P as in 'puppy'

F as in 'fat'

a horned snake

M as in 'mother'

an owl

N as in 'no'

water

R as in 'rat'

mouth

H as in 'hut'

reed shelter seen from above

twisted flax

an aspirated H as in 'ha'. (This is written as $ḥ$ to distinguish it from other h sounds.)

placenta

KH or CH as in 'Loch Ness Monster' (This is written phonetically as $ḫ$)

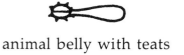

animal belly with teats

CH as 'ich' (written phonetically as $ẖ$) There is no real equivalent to this sound in English. It is like the 'ch' in German *ich*.

folded cloth or a door bolt   s as in 'sit'

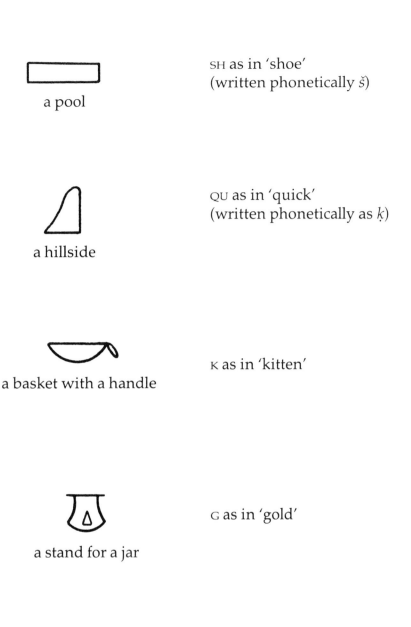

a pool

SH as in 'shoe'
(written phonetically š)

a hillside

QU as in 'quick'
(written phonetically as ḳ)

a basket with a handle

K as in 'kitten'

a stand for a jar

G as in 'gold'

a loaf of bread

T as in 'tomb'

a rope

TJ or CH as in 'chair'
(written as _t_)

a hand

D as in 'dirt'

a snake

DJ as in 'edge'
(written as _d_)

All hieroglyphs can be divided into three categories: sound signs which we call phonograms, ideograms which are both sound and sense signs, and determinatives which are sense signs that cannot be pronounced because they have no sound.

As explained before there are twenty-four hieroglyphs that represent a single sound, as shown above. There are, however, many other phonograms that represent combinations of two or more consonants. Some of the many representing two consonants are listed on the following pages.

is n+b or *nb* meaning 'every' and 'lord', and 'possessor of'. It is pronounced *neb*. As the ancient Egyptians did not write vowels, we usually provide a short 'e', as in 'met', between the consonants to help pronunciation.

is p+r or *pr* (pronounced *per*) meaning 'house'.

is d̲+w or *d̲w* (pronounced *jew*) meaning 'mountain'.

is m+n or *mn* (pronounced *men*) meaning 'established' and 'remain'.

is m+s or *ms* (pronounced *mes*) meaning 'give birth' or 'be born'.

There are other phonograms or sound signs that stand for three consonants. For example:

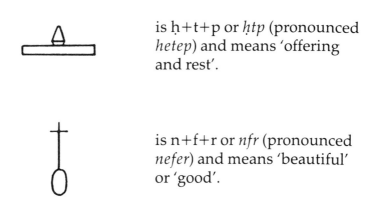

is h+t+p or *ḥtp* (pronounced *hetep*) and means 'offering and rest'.

is n+f+r or *nfr* (pronounced *nefer*) and means 'beautiful' or 'good'.

There are also many other three-consonant phonograms.

The second group of hieroglyphs is called ideograms. Ideograms are sense signs that depict exactly what they mean. Each ideogram stands for a word and can be pronounced.

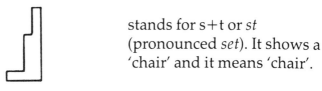

stands for s+t or *st* (pronounced *set*). It shows a 'chair' and it means 'chair'.

stands for n+w+t or *nwt* (pronounced *newt*). It shows the crossroads in the centre of town and means 'town'.

stands for w+s+r or *wsr*
(pronounced *weser*) and
means 'powerful'.

An ideogram can also signify an idea closely associated
with the object depicted which would otherwise be difficult to illustrate. For example

 means 'sun' or 'light' and
can also represent 'day' or
'time'.

 A scribe's writing
equipment can represent the
word 'scribe' or 'write'.

Ideograms can act as determinatives for words spelled
out phonetically. Determinatives are the third group
of hieroglyphs. They are placed at the end of the
alphabetic hieroglyphs to indicate the general sense
preceeding it.

For example:

is composed of:

| 1. | 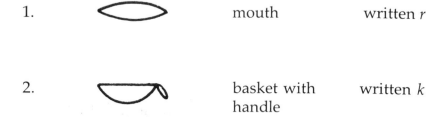 | mouth | written *r* |

| 2. | | basket with handle | written *k* |

| 3. | | determinative of sun |

The whole word is written *rk* (pronounced *rek*) and means 'time'.

is composed of:

| 1. | | quail chick | written *w* |

| 2. | | foot | written *b* |

3.  water   written *n*

4.  determinative of sun

The word is written *wbn* (pronounced *weben*) and means 'shine'.

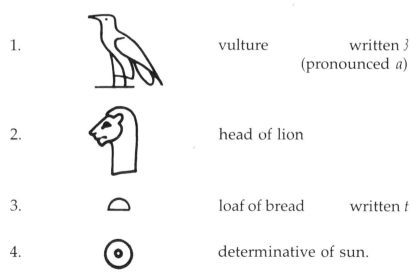

is composed of

1. vulture   written *ȝ* (pronounced *a*)

2. head of lion

3. loaf of bread   written *t*

4. determinative of sun.

The word is written *ȝt* (pronounced *at*) and means 'moment'. The lion's head is a semi-ideogram which is also read *ȝt*.

is composed of

1.   twisted flax   written *ḥ*
                    (pronounced *h*)

2.   snake   written *ḏ*
             (pronounced *dj*)

3.   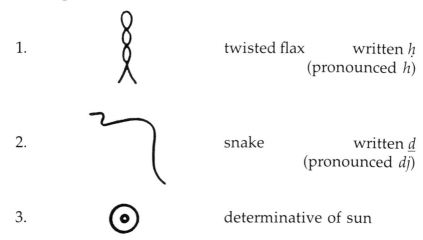 determinative of sun

The word is written *ḥḏ* (pronounced *hedge*) and means 'be bright'.

is composed of

1.   quail chick   written *w*

2.   mouth   written *r*

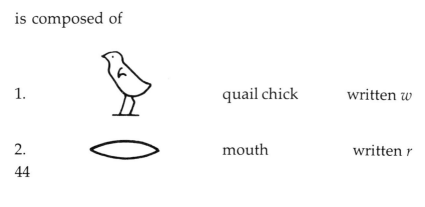

3. 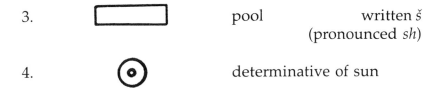 pool   written š
            (pronounced *sh*)

4.    determinative of sun

It is written *wrš* (pronounced *weresh*) and means 'spend one's time'.

A boat on water can be used as a determinative for words like:

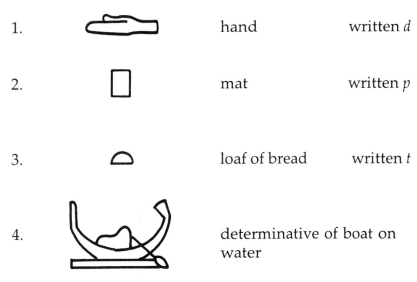

This is composed of:

1.   hand   written *d*

2.   mat   written *p*

3.   loaf of bread   written *t*

4.   determinative of boat on water

The whole word is written *dpt* (pronounced *depet*) and means 'boat'.

45

is composed of:

1. placenta   written *ḫ*
   (pronounced *ch* or *kh̆*)

2. hand   written *d*

3. determinative of boat on water

It is written *ḫd* (pronounced *khed*) and means 'sail north'.

is composed of

1. new-born antelope   written *iw* (pronounced *you*)

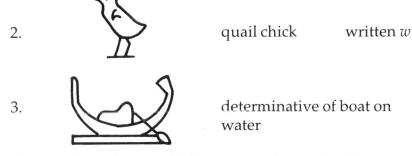

2.   quail chick   written *w*

3.   determinative of boat on water

The word is written *iw(y)* (pronounced *youee*) and means 'be boatless'.

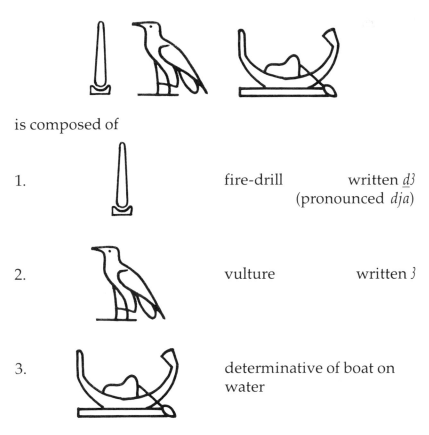

is composed of

1.   fire-drill   written *ḏꜣ* (pronounced *dja*)

2.   vulture   written *ꜣ*

3.   determinative of boat on water

The word is written *ḏꜣ(i)* (pronounced *djai*) and means 'to cross'.

Determinatives have no sound and therefore cannot be pronounced. Sometimes in the case of words of the same sound only the determinative makes clear the meaning intended. Since scribes did not write vowels, many words in Egyptian have more than one meaning. For example, in English 'c' + 't' could be read 'cat' or 'cot', and 's' and 'n' could be read 'son' or 'sun'. By adding a determinative at the end, the meaning of the word becomes clear. In a similar way many words written in hieroglyphs look identical but have different meanings. For example:

can mean 'love', 'milk jar', or 'bind'.

The first sign shows the hoe, is written *mr*, and is pronounced *mer*. The second sign shows the mouth, stands for the letter 'r' and has the sound of *r*. By adding the determinative of the 'man with his hand to his head' to the word, it takes the meaning 'love'.

If the determinative of the 'jar' to the word, is added, it becomes 'milk jar'.

By adding the determinative 'cloth' to the word it becomes 'to bind'.

Another example is the word:

It can mean 'jar', 'jubilation', 'associates' or 'waves'. It is made up of four signs, three of which are alphabetic.

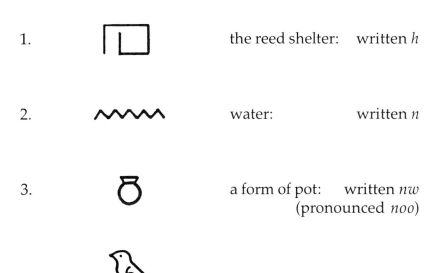

1.		the reed shelter:	written *h*
2.		water:	written *n*
3.		a form of pot:	written *nw* (pronounced *noo*)
4.		quail chick:	written *w* (pronounced *oo*)

The whole word reads *hnw* (not *hnnww!*) and is pronounced *henoo*. By adding the determinative of a 'jar' to the word it means 'jar':

By adding the determinative of a 'man with arms raised in praise' the word becomes 'jubilation':

By adding the determinative for 'people' and plural strokes, it becomes 'associates':

By adding the determinative for 'water' it becomes 'waves':

Determinatives also show where some words end, since Egyptians did not use punctuation in ancient times. There are hundreds of other determinatives that depict all kinds of things, such as human beings, animals, birds, fish, buildings, ships, trees, and plants. The following determinatives are concerned with sky, earth and water:

 depicts the sky and determines words like ḥry (pronounced hery), meaning 'to be over' and ꜥḥ(pronounced akh), meaning 'to raise up'.

 represents night and determines words like kkw (pronounced keku), meaning 'darkness'.

 represents rain and determines words like iꜣdt (pronounced yadet), meaning 'dew'.

 represents hill-country and is used to determine words like iꜣbtt (pronounced yabtet), meaning 'east', or the names of foreign countries, like Rṯnw (pronounced Retjenu), meaning 'Syria'.

These determinatives have to do with nature:

 shows a tree and determines words like *nht* (pronounced *nehet*), meaning 'sycamore'

 shows a plant or flower, and determines words like *i3rw* (pronounced *yaru*) meaning 'reeds'

 shows a vine on props and determines words like *irp* (pronounced *irep*) meaning 'wine'

 shows a branch, and determines words like *hbny* (pronounced *hebny*), meaning 'ebony', or *wh3* (pronounced *wekha*) meaning '(wooden) column'

 represents a sail, and determines words like *t3w* (pronounced *tjau*), meaning 'breath' or *mḥyt* (pronounced *mekhit*), meaning 'north wind'

Here are determinatives of people:

 a man striking with a stick, used as a determinative for words denoting activity or forceful action

 a seated woman, used to determine any female word, like 'wife', 'daughter', 'female servant' or 'musician-priestess'

 bent man leaning on a stick, used to determine words connected with age or rank

 a man steadying a basket on his head, used to determine words like *k3t* (pronounced *cat*), meaning 'labour'

 a woman sitting on a chair and holding a child, used to determine words like *rnn* (pronounced *renen*), meaning 'to nurse'

A child, used to determine words connected with youth

If you turn back to p.48 and look again at the word for 'love', 'milk jar' or 'bind' you will notice that the hieroglyphs used are:

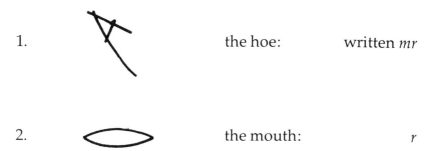

1.   the hoe: written *mr*

2.   the mouth: *r*

However, the word is not pronounced *mrr* (*merer*) but simply *mr* (*mer*). In the same way the word *hnw* is made of:

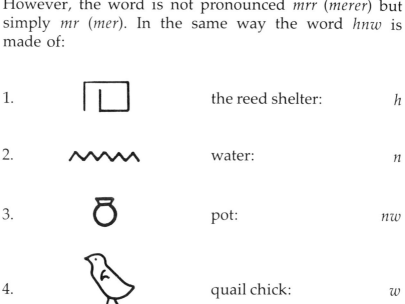

1.   the reed shelter: *h*

2.   water: *n*

3.   pot: *nw*

4.   quail chick: *w*

Instead of being read as *hnnww*, this word is actually *hnw* (pronounced *henoo*).

In both of these examples there are extra signs which we call 'phonetic complements'. Hieroglyphs of more than one consonant (like *mr*, or *nw*) can be accompanied by these phonetic complements, which express part or all of their sound, but are not actually pronounced. In words like *henoo* and *mer* it is really quite unnecessary to use phonetic complements, but in words written with a hieroglyphic sign which can be pronounced more than one way it is very necessary. For example, the sign:

a chisel, can be read as *mr* or *3b*. The phonetic complement makes it clear which reading is to be used:

mr (*mer*), meaning 'pyramid' or 'to be sick', depending on which determinative is used

3b (*ab*), meaning 'cease', 'panther' or 'desire', depending on the determinative.

26. *Superbly detailed hieroglyphs on the limestone stela of the Royal Libationer Iry. From Giza, 5th Dynasty, about 2400 BC.*

Hieroglyphs can be written so as to be read from right to left, left to right or in a column from top to bottom.

The word above reads *bin*, which means 'bad'. Here it is written from left to right. However, the ancient Egyptian more often wrote from right to left or from top to bottom:

horizontal, right to left

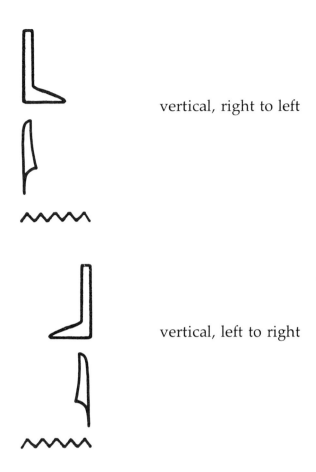

vertical, right to left

vertical, left to right

Whichever way it is written, it is always read as *bin*. There are rules for reading that are seldom broken, so that we know in which direction the hieroglyphs should be read:
1. If a text is written horizontally, always read into the eyes of the human beings and animals in the sentence. If there are no animals, look to see which direction the object is facing and read into it. (If you look at the example below, you know you must read it from right to left, because the foot is facing right.)

2. If the text is written vertically, always read from top to bottom.

There are other rules for drawing hieroglyphs. Groups of hieroglyphs are always drawn as though to fit into an invisible square, without leaving unsightly gaps. Some hieroglyphs are always drawn to fit into the entire square:

Tall hieroglyphs provide the height of the square.

Horizontal hieroglyphs provide its width.

Sometimes the order of the signs in a word is altered so that signs might be arranged more artistically. Thus:

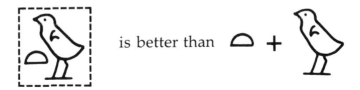

is better than

and can be read *tw* or *wt* as necessary.

is the usual writing for *ḥr-ḥb*, 'lector priest'.

The names of kings were usually accompanied by certain signs which magically granted good luck or protection, as shown in an inscription of King Sety I (27; see also 7, 28 and 30).

Means 'life, prosperity, and health' and is pronounced *ankh, wedja, seneb*. It is made up of three words:

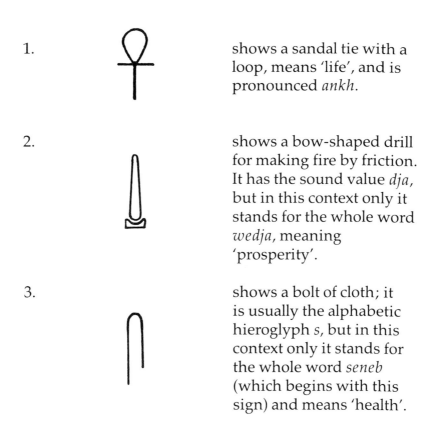

1. shows a sandal tie with a loop, means 'life', and is pronounced *ankh*.

2. shows a bow-shaped drill for making fire by friction. It has the sound value *dja*, but in this context only it stands for the whole word *wedja*, meaning 'prosperity'.

3. shows a bolt of cloth; it is usually the alphabetic hieroglyph *s*, but in this context only it stands for the whole word *seneb* (which begins with this sign) and means 'health'.

The ancient Egyptians used this formula in inscriptions to make sure that their rulers would have life, prosperity, and health for eternity.

Other hieroglyphs which often occur are:

meaning 'given life' and pronounced *dee ankh*. It is made up of:

1.   is the sign depicting bread (bread is a common offering), is pronounced *dee* and is the verb 'give'.

2.   is the sign depicting a sandal's tie-straps, is pronounced *ankh* and means 'life'.

Dee ankh was written most often after a king's name (28) and was meant to guarantee that he would live forever in the next world.

27. Upper part of a limestone relief naming King Sety I and the god Harendotes, with many hieroglyphs embodying good wishes and protection. From Abydos; 19th Dynasty, about 1310 BC.

61

28. *Part of a painted limestone stela with the figure of King Tuthmosis III; above are two of his names written in cartouches, his titles and hieroglyphs embodying good wishes. From Wadi Halfa; 18th Dynasty, about 1469 BC.*

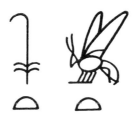

means 'king of Upper and Lower Egypt' and is pronounced *nesew bity*. This was one of the titles which usually accompanied the king's name in inscriptions (28, 30). It is composed of:

1. depicting the sedge plant, which grew in Upper Egypt, and written *sw* (pronounced *soo*).

2.  depicting the loaf of bread, and has the sound of 't'. Together, but only in this context, *sw* and *t* are pronounced *nesew*, and mean 'King of Upper Egypt'.

3. depicting a bee with the loaf of bread; together the signs are *bee tee*, and mean the 'King of Lower Egypt'. (The bee was symbolic of Lower Egypt.)

There are certain other groups of hieroglyphs that are very common.

is a 'boon which the king gives'. It is composed of three words:

1. 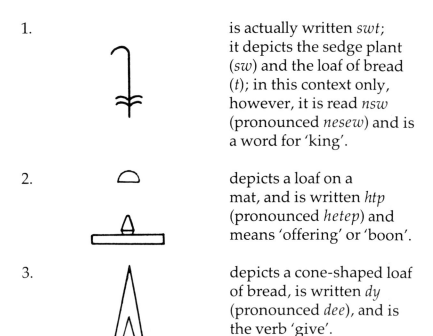 is actually written *swt*; it depicts the sedge plant (*sw*) and the loaf of bread (*t*); in this context only, however, it is read *nsw* (pronounced *nesew*) and is a word for 'king'.

2. depicts a loaf on a mat, and is written *htp* (pronounced *hetep*) and means 'offering' or 'boon'.

3. depicts a cone-shaped loaf of bread, is written *dy* (pronounced *dee*), and is the verb 'give'.

Together, the words are pronounced *hetep dee nesew*. The phrase is read in a slightly different order from that in which it is written.

Or when written from right to left:

29. Limestone stela topped by the eyes of the falcon-god and
showing the offering formula twice: the inscription on the left
invokes the funerary god Ptah-Sokaris-Osiris, that on the right,
the goddess Hathor. Second Intermediate Period, about
1633–1567 BC.

'A boon which the king gives' is the beginning of a prayer that the ancient Egyptians wrote on their tombs, coffins, and stelae (29). It means that in order to show favour to one of his subjects, the king has given offerings to a god so that the god will provide the favoured subject with everything he needs for his life after death.

Now that you have learned the alphabet and some of the rules for reading hieroglyphs, you can begin writing. Start with writing your name, placing it, as the Egyptian kings and queens did, in a cartouche (the oval ring that surrounds a royal name). You can write it vertically or horizontally and from left to right or from right to left. Cartouches invariably contain the name of a king or queen, sometimes a god, carved or painted on sculpture, on stelae, on jewellery, on coffins, on everyday objects, and on walls of temples and tombs (30, 31).

30. Part of a limestone relief containing some of the names and epithets of King Ammenemes III. The cartouche contains the name Ammenemes written in hieroglyphs. From Hawara; 12th Dynasty, reign of Ammenemes III, about 1800 BC.

31. *Sandstone statue of King Sety II inscribed with his names in cartouches around the plinth and on the shoulders. From Karnak; 19th Dynasty, about 1216-1210 BC.*

Writing numbers

The ancient Egyptians also had a special system of writing numbers.

| | 1 is shown by drawing a stroke

∩ 10 is shown by drawing a hobble for cattle

ϙ 100 is shown by drawing a coil of rope (see 14)

1,000 is shown by drawing a lotus plant (see 14)

10,000 is shown by drawing a finger

100,000 is shown by drawing a tadpole. (The ancient Egyptian probably chose the tadpole to show 100,000 because there are always so many of them swimming together.)

1,000,000 is shown by drawing the figure of a god with his arms raised over his head.

There are rules for reading and writing numbers in hieroglyphs:

1. The higher number is always written in front of the lower number.

2. When there is more than one row of numbers, start at the top and read down.

All numbers were written by using combinations of these figures. For instance, 125 is written in Egyptian numbers:

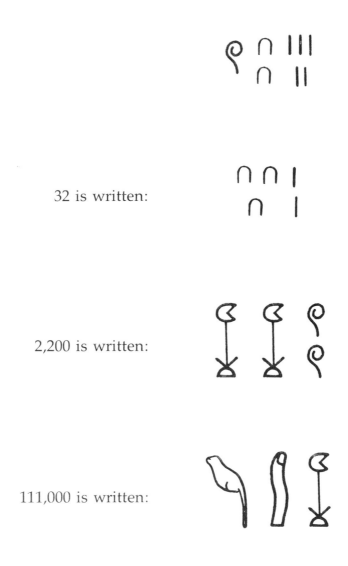

32 is written:

2,200 is written:

111,000 is written:

You can see many of these numbers on an offering list of King Ramesses III (32).

32. *Building inscription on the 3rd pylon, in which King Amenophis III lists (centre) among his gifts to Amun 4,820 deben of turquoise and 6,823 deben of jasper. Karnak; 18th Dynasty, about 1400 BC.*

Amulets

Some amulets, or good luck charms, were in the shape of hieroglyphs. The ancient Egyptians wore them as jewellery and tied these charms to their wrists, neck, ankles or waist, because they believed that the amulets had magical powers and would protect them from dangerous creatures such as crocodiles, snakes or scorpions, and from disasters such as storms, floods, accidents, disease or hunger.

Amulets were made of wood, metal and various semi-precious stones such as carnelian, turquoise and lapis lazuli. But the material most often used was faience, which was crushed quartz sand coated with glaze and fired to look like a semi-precious stone. Amulets were worn not only by the living but were also placed inside the linen wrappings of the dead to help them on their voyage to the next life. These amulets

71

used with the dead were often made of less sturdy materials, cheap substitutes for hard stone, such as thin layers of metal foil or plaster, as they did not have to suffer the wear and tear of everyday life. Here are some of the amulets that were most commmonly worn:

The *udjat* ('Eye of Horus') hieroglyph represents the eye of the falcon-headed god Horus (33). It is a combination of the human eye and the markings of a falcon's eye, the black feathers shown under the eye. It was used as an amulet against injury. According to a myth, the eye of the god Horus was ripped out of his head by the wicked storm god Seth. Later it was miraculously restored to Horus by the god Thoth.

The hieroglyph *djed* represents a column of trimmed papyrus stalks tied together or a tree-trunk with lopped-off branches (34), but later the Egyptians identified it with the backbone of the god Osiris. It is the sign of stability.

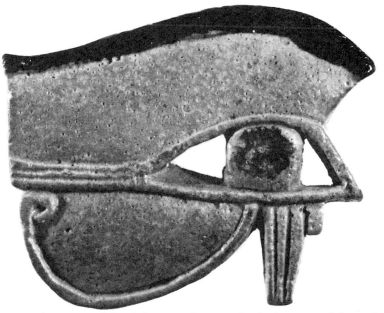

33. Udjat-eye of the falcon-god, a particularly powerful amulet. Glazed composition (faience). Late Period, about 600 BC.

The *sa* sign represents a life-preserver made out of papyrus. It was worn by the herdsman driving his animals through the swamp and protected him in case he fell into the water. As an amulet the *sa* sign was worn as a general protection against unfriendly forces.

34. Amulet in the shape of a djed *pillar. Glazed composition (faience). Late Period, about 600* BC.

The 'fish' sign provided
magical powers of
protection against
drowning (35). Sometimes
it was worn by young girls
on the end of their
pigtails. It was also the
good luck charm of
boatmen.

*35. Amulet as jewellery in the form of a fish, which gave protection
to children against drowning and was worn at the end of a plait.
Gold inlaid with green felspar. 12th Dynasty, about 1900-1800 BC.*

The *ankh* sign, as
described before,
represents a sandal tie
with a loop. It means 'life'
and therefore has more
power than almost any
other hieroglyph.

Hieroglyphs in amuletic form offer a glimpse into the
richness of the ancient Egyptian civilisation. This book
has shown just a small part of what there is to learn
about ancient Egypt, its writing and its language, and
will perhaps encourage you to study further.

75

Some important rulers and their dynasties

Archaic Period
First Dynasty (3100-2890 BC)
NARMER

Second Dynasty (2890-2686 BC)
PERIBSEN
KHASEKHEMWY

Old Kingdom
Third Dynasty (2686-2613 BC)
DJOSER

Fourth Dynasty (2613-2494 BC)
CHEOPS
CHEPHREN
MYCERINUS

Fifth Dynasty (2494-2345 BC)
USERKAF
DJEDKARE ISESI
WENIS

Sixth Dynasty (2345-2181 BC)
TETI
PEPY I
PEPY II

First Intermediate Period
Seventh – Tenth Dynasties (2181-2133 BC)
This was a troubled period, in which Egypt was divided into many small kingdoms, each with a different ruler.

Middle Kingdom
Eleventh Dynasty (2133-1991 BC)

Twelfth Dynasty (1991-1786 BC)
AMMENEMES I
SESOSTRIS I
AMMENEMES II
SESOSTRIS II
SESOSTRIS III
AMMENEMES III

Thirteenth Dynasty (1786-1633 BC)
SOBKHOTEP III

Second Intermediate Period (1633-1567 BC)
Many kings ruled Egypt in this period, including two
foreign dynasties known as the Hyksos kings.

New Kingdom
Eighteenth Dynasty (1567-1320 BC)
AMENOPHIS I
TUTHMOSIS I
TUTHMOSIS II
QUEEN HATSHEPSUT
TUTHMOSIS III
AMENOPHIS II
TUTHMOSIS IV
AMENOPHIS III
AMENOPHIS IV (AKHENATEN)
TUTANKHAMUN

Nineteenth Dynasty (1320-1200 BC)
SETY I
RAMESSES II

Twentieth Dynasty (1200-1085 BC)
RAMESSES III

Third Intermediate Period (1085-750 BC)
This was again a period of many kings; those in the
north were weak; in the south priests acted as kings.

Late Period
Twenty-Fifth Dynasty (Kings from Nubia)
(747-656 BC)
  TAHARQA

Twenty-Sixth Dynasty (664-525 BC)
  AMASIS
  PSAMMETICHUS III

Twenty-Seventh Dynasty (Kings from Persia)
(525-404 BC)
  DARIUS I

Thirtieth Dynasty (380-343 BC)
  NECTANEBO I, II
  ALEXANDER THE GREAT (332-323 BC)

Ptolemaic Period (323-30 BC)
  PTOLEMY I-XII
  CLEOPATRA VII

References to the Illustrations

Most of the objects illustrated in this book are in the British Museum. Their Departmental Collection numbers are listed below. Illustration nos 5 and 32 are by Carol Andrews; all others are copyright of the British Museum.

1. BM 5337	20. BM 1168
2,3. BM 24	21. BM 9999, sheet 22
4. BM 32	22. BM 69098
6. BM 2	23. BM 1514
7. BM 1519	24. BM 38504
8. BM 55724	25. BM 38276
9. BM 32693	26. BM 1168
10. BM 24428	27. BM 609
12. BM 579	28. BM 1021
13. BM 586	29. BM 197
14. BM 1242	30. BM 1072
15. BM 886	31. BM 26
16. BM 1848	33. BM 23092
17. BM 30840	34. BM 12235
18. BM 26706	35. BM 30484
19. BM 12784, 5512	*Front cover* BM 117

Index

The figures in italic refer to illustrations